MEDIEVAL CASTLE

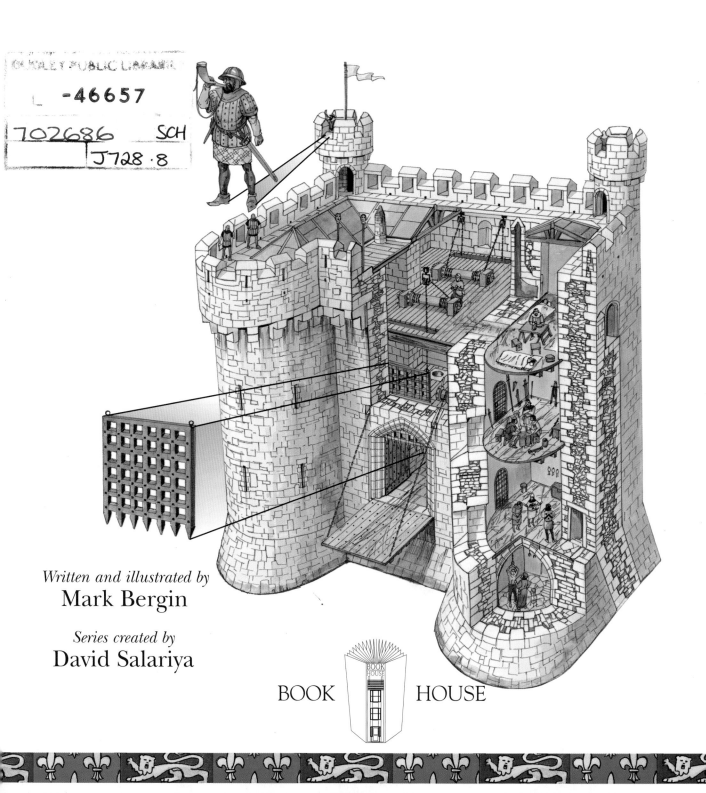

Written and illustrated by
Mark Bergin

Series created by
David Salariya

BOOK HOUSE

THE AGE OF CASTLES

EUROPE WAS TORN APART by wars and feuds throughout the Middle Ages – the period between about AD 1000 and 1450. Conflicts were usually attempts to plunder or gain neighbouring territories. Hundreds of fortresses and castles were built for protection against enemy armies and as homes for lords and their followers. From these strongholds, warrior kings and barons could command and control the land over which they ruled.

Castles were built on sites that were easy to defend, such as steep hillsides or rocky outcrops, or places such as river crossings and major road routes where it was easier to control trade and access to land. Some castles were impressive sights, towering over the landscape, a physical reminder of the power and influence of the ruling classes.

FEUDAL SYSTEM

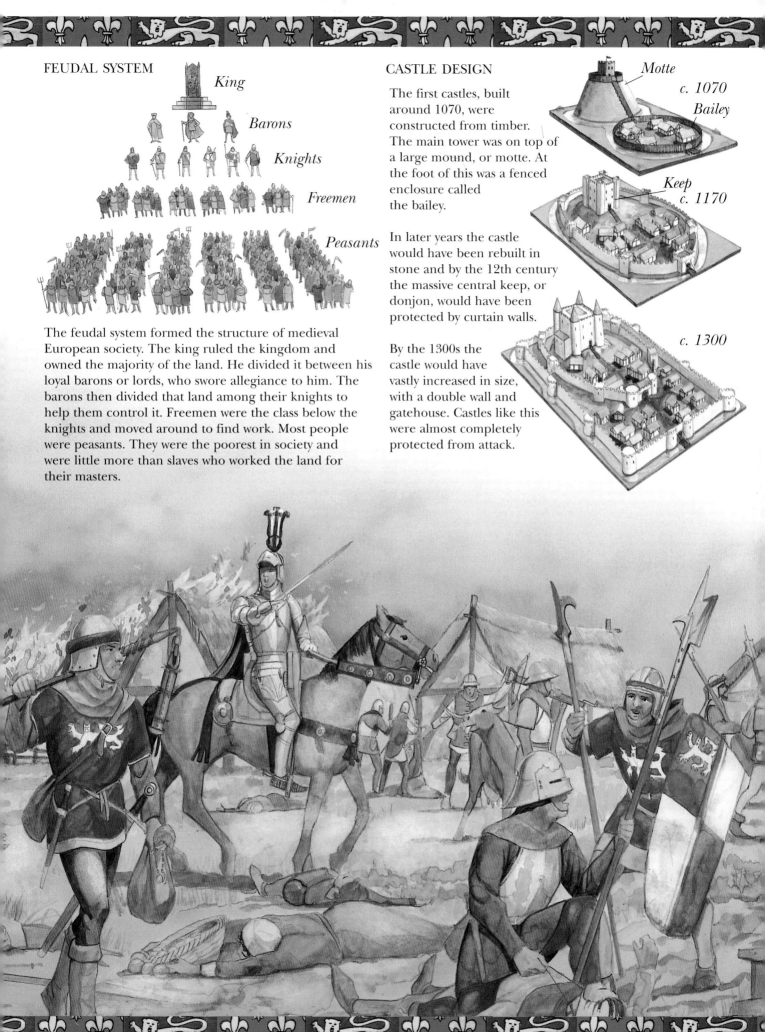

King

Barons

Knights

Freemen

Peasants

The feudal system formed the structure of medieval European society. The king ruled the kingdom and owned the majority of the land. He divided it between his loyal barons or lords, who swore allegiance to him. The barons then divided that land among their knights to help them control it. Freemen were the class below the knights and moved around to find work. Most people were peasants. They were the poorest in society and were little more than slaves who worked the land for their masters.

CASTLE DESIGN

The first castles, built around 1070, were constructed from timber. The main tower was on top of a large mound, or motte. At the foot of this was a fenced enclosure called the bailey.

In later years the castle would have been rebuilt in stone and by the 12th century the massive central keep, or donjon, would have been protected by curtain walls.

By the 1300s the castle would have vastly increased in size, with a double wall and gatehouse. Castles like this were almost completely protected from attack.

Motte

Bailey

c. 1070

Keep

c. 1170

c. 1300

BUILDING A CASTLE

A CRAFTSMAN'S DAY

The master mason discussed the progress of each section of wall. He allocated work for the day to the various craftsmen and labourers.

The early timber castles and their earthworks were constructed relatively quickly and cheaply. During a war campaign a wooden castle could be raised in an amazing eight days! A vast amount of timber was needed to build a large castle. The fortress of Telleborg, in Denmark, was built from about 8,000 oak trees. In the 12th century only the most powerful and wealthy lords could afford to build a stone castle. The building materials, including the stone, timber and iron were sometimes brought great distances to the site. Skilled craftsmen and unskilled labourers were needed to create such huge fortresses and as many as 3,000 men were employed. The master mason was in charge of building operations and he was often highly paid. He surveyed potential sites, drew up plans and ordered materials. He also hired the workforce and supervised the freemasons and journeymen who cut and shaped the stone. The site of a new castle was extremely important and was always chosen with care. A source of clean drinking water was essential. Castles had to provide a home for the lord and lady, quarters for their servants and soldiers, storerooms and dungeons. In a siege the castle needed to be able to provide all its inhabitants with shelter, food and fuel, perhaps for months at a time.

Stone was transported by cart from local quarries when possible. However, for some English castles stone was imported from France by ship.

The walls were made like a sandwich – fine-trimmed blocks were used on the inside and outside surfaces and the middle was filled with a rough limestone rubble concrete.

Rough timber was cut with a two-man long saw (right). Wood was sometimes toughened by soaking it in water over winter. The roof beams were held together by wooden pegs.

Two-man long saw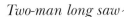

Freemason

A rough mason, or banker, was the lowest form of stonemason. The banker cut simple shapes for a freemason (left) to shape into a finished piece of masonry. Freemasons were skilled men who cut stone into the shapes required for walls, staircases, arrow loops and decorative arches and vaults. Smoothed and cut stone was called ashlar.

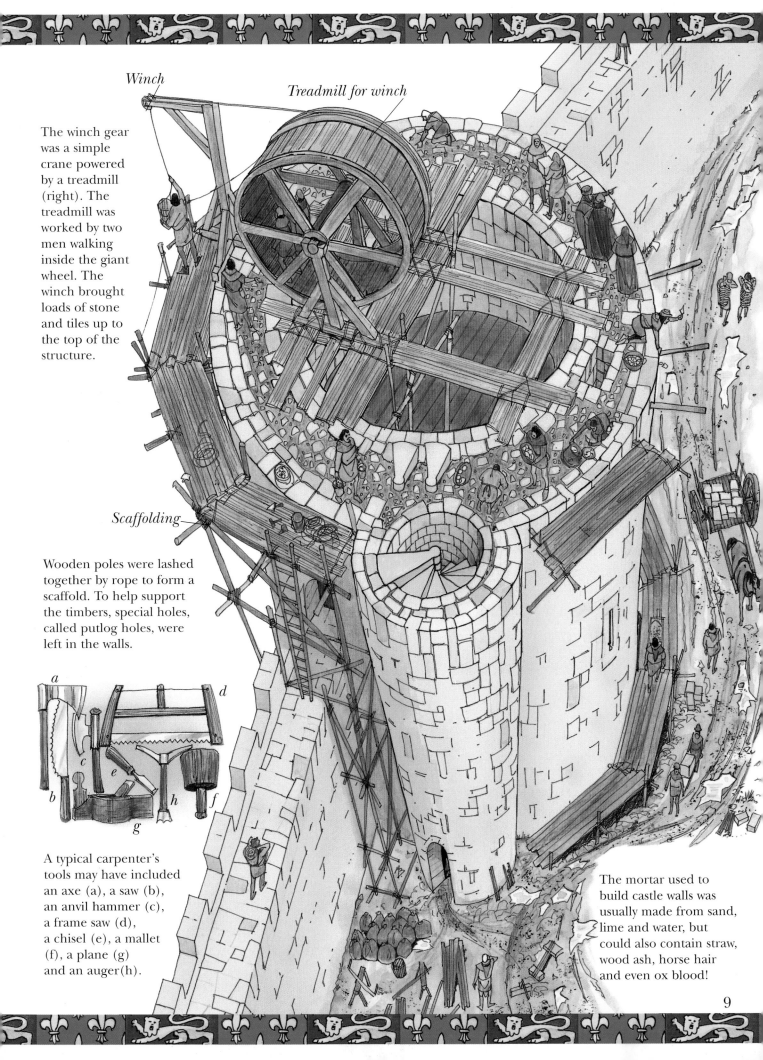

Winch

Treadmill for winch

The winch gear was a simple crane powered by a treadmill (right). The treadmill was worked by two men walking inside the giant wheel. The winch brought loads of stone and tiles up to the top of the structure.

Scaffolding

Wooden poles were lashed together by rope to form a scaffold. To help support the timbers, special holes, called putlog holes, were left in the walls.

A typical carpenter's tools may have included an axe (a), a saw (b), an anvil hammer (c), a frame saw (d), a chisel (e), a mallet (f), a plane (g) and an auger(h).

The mortar used to build castle walls was usually made from sand, lime and water, but could also contain straw, wood ash, horse hair and even ox blood!

9

A castle needed clear views of the surrounding countryside in all directions, so hilltops were favoured.

Clearing wood and undergrowth from the chosen site was the first step. The wood could be used for the first defences, gates and buildings.

Master masons did the groundwork and planned the layout of the castle keep. They also checked the foundations – wherever possible castles were built on solid rock.

As the castle grew, the original timber battlements were replaced and improved by permanent stonework.

The curtain walls had square mural towers along them to provide vantage points for lookouts to shoot enemy attackers (see pages 38-39).

The parapets (the tops of the castle walls) provided defending soldiers with a safe place to hide and shoot from.

Mural tower

Parapet

CASTLE DESIGN

BY 1350, CASTLE KEEPS were designed as quarters for the lord and his knights. The one or two curtain walls surrounding the keep also enclosed an area in which other buildings sprang up. These extra buildings formed a small town, catering for the needs of all who visited or worked at the castle. There would have been many workshops for tradespeople including a tailor's, a blacksmith's, potters, coopers and candlemakers. The castle stables, kitchen and garrison buildings were positioned around the inner walls. Most castles were designed to include such facilities as a well to ensure the supply of drinking water, a windmill to grind corn into flour and a church or chapel for worship. From this power base a medieval lord had everything he needed to control and rule the surrounding lands.

Many castles had their own mill tower, where local farmers could bring their corn to the miller for grinding into flour. The windmill's sails, or sweeps, could be positioned to show whether the mill was open for milling: position 'X' meant yes, but position '+'meant the mill was closed for repairs.

Windmill

Mill tower

Gatehouse

The gatehouse, even though very strongly fortified, was a weak spot (see pages 14-15).

11

Those born into a noble family had a privileged upbringing. Maids and servants saw to their every need.

Noble boys often became pages, waiting on tables and running messages for their lord.

Young noble ladies learnt French (which most people spoke in medieval Europe) and Latin.

Learning the rules of polite behaviour was required when living in noble society.

Tapestries (right) were large decorative wall-hangings made with brightly-coloured thread. They often showed hunting scenes, jousting, battles, the daily life of the lord and lady or the family's heraldic crest. Some of the best tapestries were created in the French town of Arras.

Tapestry

THE CASTLE KEEP

AT THE HEART of the castle was the keep, or donjon. It was the first part of the castle to be built in stone. The rooms in the keep included a great hall for feasting and administration, a chapel, a treasury, an archive and a storeroom. The lord and lady lived in a combination of a bedroom and sitting room called a solar. There they enjoyed a grand lifestyle with lavish food and beautiful clothes. By the 1200s castles had well-furnished bed chambers and living rooms. These were heated by large open fires and were often decorated with signs of the zodiac, folktales or biblical stories. Richly embroidered wall hangings and curtains helped to keep out draughts. At each corner of the keep was a tower with a spiral staircase. The stairs rose in a clockwise direction so that an attacking soldier climbing the stairs would find it difficult to use his sword if held in the right arm.

In the bottom third of the keep there were many storerooms, a wine cellar, a dungeon, a well and an archive. The archive housed all the important documents, paperwork and books. Books were handwritten and very expensive so they were kept locked up.

Salt cellar
Salt may have been served to the lord in a ship-shaped salt cellar. Salt was expensive and was therefore a measure of social status.

Chapel

Chaplain

The chaplain's room was where his robes and vestments were kept. The chapel was situated next to the lord's domestic quarters.

These two men (right) are measuring out spices. Imported from the Far East, spices were very expensive and used only sparingly.

Storeroom

Solar

The solar was the lord's private room. The lord's bed was the most expensive piece of furniture in the castle. The tapestry curtains were drawn to keep out draughts.

The lady of the castle was usually an expert at needlework, as was expected of well-bred medieval women. Music, weaving, embroidery and cooking were all essential skills for a noblelady.

Taking a bath in medieval times was a rare event. Ladies-in-waiting had to haul up buckets of heated water to the solar. Even a king would usually have taken a bath only once every three weeks!

Great hall

Wine cellar

Well

Archive

Marshal

The marshal was in charge of organising the lodgings around the castle. He had grooms, pages and serving maids to help him. They made sure rooms were ready for visitors.

13

THE GATEHOUSE

THE CASTLE'S GATEHOUSE was seen as a weak spot so it was very strongly fortified. A typical gatehouse had four barriers to block an enemy's way. First was the drawbridge over the moat. Made from thick planks of wood, the drawbridge could be raised quickly if an enemy approached – iron chains were attached to a winch in the room above and could be hauled up. The next barriers were two portcullises. These had sharpened, pointed ends that could spear or crush anybody unfortunate enough to get under them. In the roof area between the two portcullises were murder holes so that any enemy getting this far would be picked off by an archer above. The last barrier was a set of heavy gates. These were shut and barred from inside the castle.

The castle guards lived, ate and slept in the turrets so there was always someone on guard. Around the top of the gatehouse parapets there were many arrow loops and holes through which boiling oil or heavy stones could be dropped onto attackers below.

Guard sounding the alarm

In the small watch-turrets lookouts could sound the alarm or signal the approach of friends by various blows on a hunting horn.

The rotting heads of criminals or traitors were on view to the public as they entered the main gate, to serve as a warning.

The portcullis (below) was a heavy sliding grid made of wood with iron fittings. It was lowered down grooves cut in the gatehouse wall.

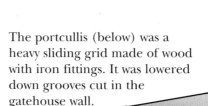

Portcullis

ENTRANCE FEATURES

A wicket gate was a small door in the main gate and was used by visitors at night or when the castle gates were shut.

Peepholes in the side of the gatehouse gave guards a chance to keep an eye on visitors as they entered the castle.

Murder holes were situated in the roof of the gatehouse between the portcullises. Arrows or stones could rain down from these on intruders.

Chimney

Chimneys began to be used in castles around the 1350s. Before that, a hole in the wall or roof allowed smoke to escape.

The winch gear that lifted the portcullis was operated by the guards. A brake on the side could be knocked out quickly to drop the barrier on intruders below.

Garrison guards (below) were on duty day and night. The lord's constable, or second-in-command, had his quarters in the gatehouse so he was always aware of who was entering and leaving the castle.

The castle's torture chamber was underneath the gatehouse. Prisoners were tortured with hot irons until they confessed to whatever they were accused of. Captured knights were often held to ransom and a large sum of money was usually demanded for their safe return.

Murder hole

Drawbridge

CASTLE RESIDENTS

A CASTLE was like a small town and numerous people were needed to run it smoothly and to serve and protect the lord and lady. The constable was in charge of the castle garrison and the daily running of the castle when the lord and lady were away. A number of foot soldiers and archers were retained, or garrisoned, to defend the castle. The chaplain held services in the castle chapel and may have acted as a secretary for the castle as he would have been one of the few people who could write. The pantler was responsible for buying food and provisions, the butler dispensed wine and a ewerer provided clean linen for use in the great hall. Young noble boys came to live at the castle to become pages and they helped to serve meals. The horses and their stables were cared for by grooms. The worst job in the castle must have been the gong farmer's – he had to clean out the pit, or gong, under the lavatories! All these people kept the castle well maintained, safe and comfortable.

Jester • Soldier • Lady's servant • Bailiff • Marshal • Servant • Page • Cook • Ewerer • Falconer • Knight • Reeve

Several administrators looked after the castle's business. Clerks kept the castle accounts and a steward was in charge of the household. Bailiffs collected rents from tenants and a reeve managed the lord's farms and estates.

CRAFTS IN THE CASTLE

Glass was specially made for tableware on the lord's table and stained glass for decorative windows.

Tailors made the lord and lady fine clothes with imported silk or other expensive materials.

Silversmiths and goldsmiths worked on tableware and jewellery for the castle and its chapel.

Painters decorated the furniture and walls with murals of daily life, biblical scenes and signs of the zodiac.

Jewellers worked on special commissions for the lord and the chaplain.

Weavers made the cloth from which the castle staff's clothes were fashioned.

The blacksmith was always busy making and reparing horseshoes, tools and farm implements.

Potters created tableware and storage pots for the whole castle community.

Cobblers made beautiful shoes for the nobles as well as boots for the garrison soldiers.

Masons crafted the decorative stonework in the church and castle.

Stained glass was used in churches to portray biblical figures and stories.

Carpenters made complete frameworks for buildings. They also did the fine carving on church furniture.

Fine tapesteries were skilfully handmade from brightly-coloured threads.

Lord of the castle

Lady

Chaplain

Groom

Constable

Archer

LIVING LIKE A LORD

IN PEACETIME, the lord and lady had a lavish lifestyle, hunting, hawking and entertaining other nobles. The lord also oversaw the running of his estates, such as inspecting the annual accounts drawn up by his steward and bailiff. He dealt with such documents as petitions from villagers explaining why they could not pay their taxes. Merchants from overseas sent letters asking for permission to trade in the lord's domain. If the lord was away, the running of the castle fell to his wife. From an early age, noblewomen were taught to manage large households, to give orders to servants and to keep accounts. The lady also had to organise the defence of the castle if it was attacked while her husband was absent.

LORDS' AND LADIES' CLOTHING

Lords and ladies wore fashionable clothes (below) made of dyed wool or expensive silk and velvet embroidered and trimmed with fur. Elaborate headdresses were fashionable among the upper classes in the Middle Ages. Men and women both wore jewellery and gloves and perfumed their hair.

HUNTING AND HAWKING

Medieval nobles enjoyed hunting and hawking. These activities could last an entire day and were good exercise for horses and their riders. Wild boar, deer, foxes, hares and rabbits provided sport and meat for the castle larder. The lord's hunting dogs were specially bred and carefully trained to smell out and track down their quarry. These dogs were usually valuable and were cared for by the lord's huntsmen and kennel-grooms. Ladies generally preferred hawking to hunting, often riding into the forest and taking a picnic. The lord's falconer was highly skilled in training and flying his birds of prey, such as peregrine falcons.

Hunting wild boar

ADMINISTERING JUSTICE

The lord of the castle sat in judgement in the great hall each morning. He listened to tenants' disputes, crimes or rent troubles. The chaplain kept a careful record of the cases, judgements and the punishments given in a ledger. The treasurer collected punishment fines and used the money to pay soldiers and other household expenses.

If someone was found guilty of a crime, the lord decided the punishment immediately. A thief or someone who had committed a violent act could be whipped or even hanged. For those found to be traitors against the king, punishment was extreme – the person was hung, then drawn (dragged by horses) before being quartered (cut into four pieces)! The head of the traitor was then boiled, tarred and stuck on a spike on the gatehouse for all to see.

DUBBING OF KNIGHTS

One of the lord's duties was to dub knights. Squires could only become fully-fledged knights when they attained the high standards required and this usually happened around the age of 21. The squire swore an oath of loyalty to his lord and the king. The lord 'dubbed' the squire by tapping his shoulders with a sword. The squire was then a knight.

TAX COLLECTION

The lord had the power to tax his tenants in many ways. If he needed to raise money to go on a war campaign for the king, he may put up town taxes. These taxes would filter down to the peasants in the form of higher priced goods and food. Collecting taxes (right) was normally the job of the steward. He was well-paid for his responsibilities which included collecting taxes, organising farm workers, keeping accounts and informing the treasury how much to pay for expenses and wages.

Barracks, Armoury and Stables

SOME LATER CASTLE DESIGNS included barracks. The castle at Carcassonne, in France, in the 13th century included barracks. The barracks housed the castle garrison, made up of foot soldiers, archers and hired soldiers. They ate, slept and spent their spare time in the barracks. The captain of the guard had his own room but was close enough to keep an eye on the men under his command. Weapons and armour were made and maintained in the castle armoury. Both master craftsmen and apprentices worked in the armoury, cutting and hammering sheets of heated metal into swords, helmets and shields (below). If a knight was to survive in battle he needed good quality, well-fitting and often expensive armour. During this period the very best armour came from the German cities of Nuremberg and Augsburg or Milan in Italy.

Bowmen (right) were well paid, skilful and essential members of the castle garrison. Crossbows were lethal – bolts could pierce full armour at 50 m! Their only disadvantage was the time it took to reload. For this reason crossbows tended to be used in castle and siege warfare, where bowmen were able to shelter behind battlements while preparing to fire.

Captain of the guard preparing for duty

CHAIN MAIL

Early chain mail was made up of many interlocking rings of iron, skilfully made into coats or leggings (below left). By the 13th century armoured coats were made from overlapping metal plates or sections (below right).

In the armoury workshop, a grindstone of granite was used to give swords, axes and lances a straight, sharp edge (below).

Chain mail from the 11th century

13th-century 'coat of plates'

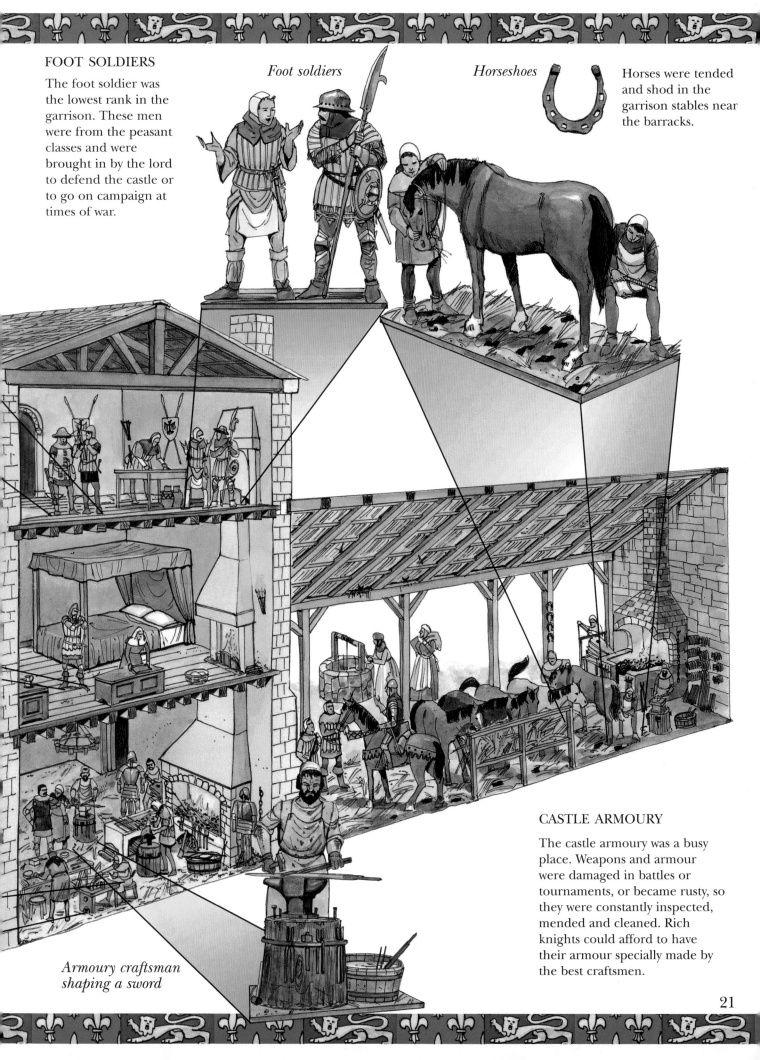

FOOT SOLDIERS

The foot soldier was the lowest rank in the garrison. These men were from the peasant classes and were brought in by the lord to defend the castle or to go on campaign at times of war.

Foot soldiers

Horseshoes

Horses were tended and shod in the garrison stables near the barracks.

Armoury craftsman shaping a sword

CASTLE ARMOURY

The castle armoury was a busy place. Weapons and armour were damaged in battles or tournaments, or became rusty, so they were constantly inspected, mended and cleaned. Rich knights could afford to have their armour specially made by the best craftsmen.

MEDIEVAL STREETS

THE CASTLE STREETS were hemmed into the space between the keep and the curtain walls and were crowded and noisy places. Peddlers and shopkeepers shouted about their wares, a town crier advertised forthcoming fairs and marriages and beggars called out for alms (charity given to the poor). The streets were smelly because there were no proper drains. Rubbish and human waste were thrown directly into the streets and the nearby river. Some town councils paid 'scavengers' to clear the refuse. Craftsmen, such as cobblers, had workshops in the town. Many craftsmen and merchants formed societies, or guilds, to control prices, ensure goods were of a high standard and organise the training of apprentices. On market days, held once or twice a week, travelling merchants set up stalls selling items such as candles, fresh fish, pies, pottery, glass, ale, spices and leather goods. Entertainers – musicians, jugglers, acrobats and people with trained animals – performed for a penny or less. People went to the market to buy goods, but also to meet friends and catch up on local news and gossip.

The stocks (opposite) were used as a form of public humiliation for those who committed petty crimes, such as slander. The offender's hands or feet were put in the stocks and townspeople were encouraged to throw rubbish and rotten food at him.

In the tailor's workshop seamstresses made, mended and cleaned clothes for most people in the castle. They worked on soldiers' wool-padded tunics as well as fine silk dresses for the lady of the castle.

Seamstresses in a tailor's workshop

Merchants from the East sold spices, silk, jewels and carpets. This well-dressed merchant is calling out to the crowd about his wares.

Travelling merchant

Bear and handler

Trained bears were a crowd pleaser as most people would never have had the opportunity to see a live bear before. Bears are intelligent animals and could be trained easily. This practice was cruel and often they were taken from their mother as cubs. People paid to see a bear perform tricks for its handler.

Stocks

Market stall

Travelling merchants and their market stalls sold many items not available locally, such as fine and colourful cloth from northern France (left). People haggled over prices.

Off-duty soldiers, farmers and traders could buy food and drink at the ale house, or tavern, and catch up on news and gossip (below).

Inside a tavern

A chandler, or candlemaker, made candles for the castle. The lord's candles were made from beeswax, but for peasants, tallow was used. Wicks were made from thread or thin rushes.

Food was prepared by hand. Pies often had birds' heads popping out of the crust as decoration!

Flour for the castle was ground in the lord's windmill. The miller produced different grades of flour – fine to make white bread for the lord or coarse to make brown bread for the servants.

Bread was baked in brick ovens outside the keep, in case of fire. The ovens were heated by burning wood and the loaves were laid on the hot floor using wooden shovels called peels.

Pages, squires and waiters hurried around serving food under the watchful eye of the steward. The staff wore tunics bearing the lord's heraldry (below).

Musicians (below) entertained diners with drums, lutes, fiddles, or viols, and a wooden shawm – a type of oboe. A jester circled the room making fun of the guests. Travelling bands of jugglers, acrobats or actors may also have been invited to entertain guests.

FOOD AND FEASTING

FEASTS WERE HELD on special occasions, such as festivals or when the lord received visitors. The lord and his guests sat at a table apart from the other diners and overlooking them. Important members of the household sat at tables near the lord. Less important people sat further away. The main meal was eaten at about 10 am and could last several hours. The top table was served first with silver or gold tableware. Everyone else's meals were served on thick slices of stale brown bread called trenchers. These soaked up gravy, grease and sauce from the food. Everyone used their fingers and a spoon to eat with, (forks were not in common use until the 1660s). At the end of the meal, the trenchers were given to beggars outside the castle.

Musicians

Trencher

Waiter

The lord's hunting dogs (right) roamed around the hall in search of tasty titbits, such as discarded bones.

Before any noble person ate the food, it was inspected and sampled by a food taster (right). This was to check that nothing was poisoned. The lord's table also had a ewerer to serve the wine and to provide clean linen when necessary.

Food taster

Lord's table

Wine jug

Wine and ale were served in glazed, patterned jugs and tankards.

Food for the feast was highly decorated to impress the guests. Spiced food was a sign of wealth as the cost of imported spices was very high. Cooks mixed sweet and savoury foods together: pheasants, ducks, pigs' heads, herring, salmon, whiting and sweet pies of creamed fruit all sat on the same feasting table.

Pheasant

Fruit pie

Meat was salted to preserve it and kept in huge wooden vats. Salt was expensive because it was made by evaporating sea water from shallow lagoons.

Grapes were pressed to make wine. Poorer people drank cider or ale.

A carefully-packed cauldron hung over the fire could cook many different things at the same time. Separate items were placed in the cauldron in pots or wrapped in linen.

Locally available herbs, such as parsley, borage and primrose, were commonly used in cooking.

SUPPLYING THE CASTLE

TO SUPPLY the two or three hundred residents of a castle was a huge task. Depending on the type of soil and climate, the estate's farmers grew grain or reared livestock. A well-run farm was self-sufficient and produced everything the farmer and his family needed as well as enough left to sell. The seasons controlled everyone's diet in the Middle Ages. In summer and autumn food was plentiful, but as winter approached, people ate meat and other foods that had been preserved to last through winter and spring.

Ale, or beer, did not keep well, so was brewed all year round (right). The water supply was often contaminated so everyone drank ale. Women and children drank watered down ale, called small beer.

Sheep were farmed for their wool, which was sold to weave into cloth. The money went back into the farm or paid taxes.

Shears

Farm labourer shearing a sheep

At harvest time every able-bodied man, woman and child helped to gather in the crops (below).

After the cows were milked (below), butter and cheese could be made in churns. When the cows were of a certain age they were killed for meat. The hide was made into leather goods and the horns were ideal for cups, spoons and archer's bow ends.

Ploughing teams often worked in poor conditions – oxen were difficult to handle and the primitive plough cut only a shallow furrow.

Peasants rarely ate meat – their diet was mainly milk, cheese, eggs, bread and a thick vegetable stew called pottage.

Cooking in a cauldron

Preserving meat in a barrel of salt

Before winter, beef, lamb and fish were preserved in barrels of salt (above) or by smoking. Beans, herbs and grain were dried and apples were stored but most did not last the whole winter.

TAXES

Peasants paid many forms of taxes to their lord. Even the right to collect firewood on estate land had a wood-penny tax.

Chiminage tax had to be paid for using roads passing through the lord's forests.

Tenants paid a type of rent called bolder-silver to live in a house on the lord's manor.

The lord's horses were fed by means of another tax. Peasants had to supply good feed as a tax called foddercorn.

Heriot was a type of death duty, paid by a family in the form of the dead man's best animal.

BECOMING A KNIGHT

IT TOOK YEARS OF TRAINING to become a knight. Around the age of eight, a boy from a wealthy family was sent to work as a page in a castle. He learned to read and write as well as practising good manners and social skills. If the page did well and showed promise, he was made a squire at the age of 14. He was then assigned to a knight and had to accompany him on war campaigns and to tournaments.

A nobleman's son was sent to meet the lord. He agreed to accept the boy as a page.

A young page helped serve meals, run messages and learnt the polite behaviour necessary in noble society.

At the age of 14 the page became a squire and learnt sword skills.

Hours were spent practising riding and fighting on horseback too.

A squire's duties included caring for armour and weapons and helping his knight train (below). A squire also learned to dress his knight for battle, which took around fifteen minutes.

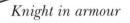

Knight in armour

Knights were trained to exercise in heavy but well-fitting and manoeuvrable armour (above) – a fit man could even run in it!

A squire learned how to dress his knight for battle.

Squires also accompanied and assisted their knights at tournaments.

At the age of 21 a good squire was able to become a knight. He spent a night praying in the castle chapel.

The squire bathed to clean his body and wash away his sins. Then he was able to start afresh as a knight.

Kneeling in front of the lord or king, the squire swore to serve him and to live by the code of chivalry.

During a squire's apprenticeship, experienced soldiers trained him in tactics and the rules of warfare. A squire also learned skills such as horse riding and how to handle a sword and lance. Managing a powerful stallion in combat was very different to the cart horse a boy may have ridden at home. The quintain (right) helped squires learn to use a lance. The rider had to hit a shield-shaped rotating target square-on with the lance. If he was off target or too slow, a weight or sack would hit him as it swung round.

Quintain

At the dubbing ceremony (left), a new knight was presented with his sword and spurs. All knights were called 'Sir'. They swore to live by the code of chivalry, to be gentle, worthy, faithful and devoted, to defend the church and protect the poor and weak from injustice.

He was then dubbed (tapped on the shoulders with a sword) by the lord or king and became a knight.

Spurs were a sign of knighthood. They were often given as a reward for bravery.

When a knight was travelling between tournaments or other events he took his squire, groom and other servants with him. They all wore the knight's colours and heraldry. Heavy armour was worn by knights in the jousting competitions at tournaments, but not in battle.

29

The frog-mouthed jousting helmet (left) was popular across medieval Europe. A jousting knight could see his opponent by leaning forward during a charge. Before collision the body straightened to stop the opponent's lance coming through the helmet's slit. The knight's heraldic crest was displayed on the top.

Before tournaments, pavilions were erected to ensure nobles and judges got the best view of the action (below). The knights had tents for their servants and armour (right).

Knight's tent

Squire

Jousting helmet

Pavilion

The prizes meant that tournaments were not just an opportunity for glory – a skilled knight could win horses, armour and money.

TOURNAMENTS

TOURNAMENTS were mock battles in which knights could show off and practise their fighting skills. By the 13th and 14th centuries these competitions were highly organised, with rules and judges. Tournament days were huge social occasions. The people of the castle manor came to watch their favourite knight, cheer him on and wear his colours. Rewards were high for the victors – defeated knights lost valuable horses or armour to their opponents.

The most common form of combat was the tilt, or joust. This contest featured knights charging at each other on horseback with lances. In later contests a tilt barrier was used, which prevented head-on collisions. Knights were often maimed or killed in a tournament. Contests between teams of knights were known as melees. There could be up to 20 on each team, all on horseback.

Knights wore specially strengthened armour to withstand the impact of a lance during jousting. Their heavy horses were bred especially for tournaments and were trained to charge.

Tournament horse

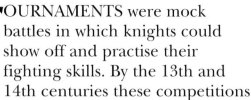

A knight on tour took with him his servants, squire and horses.

Heraldry was a complex system used to identify each knight. It used symbols and colours which appeared on every individual knight's shields and surcoats.

Squires handed out their knight's colours to supporters at tournaments. These small shields were worn in their hats before the games began.

Jousting saddles were brightly coloured and made of wood and leather. They were raised at the front and back to give the rider additional support.

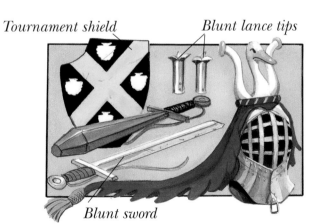

Tournament shield   *Blunt lance tips*

Blunt sword

Weapons and armour were specially made for tournaments. The metal tips of lances were splayed so that they would inflict less damage, swords were blunted and maces were made of wood. Shields had the top corner removed so that a lance could be held crossed over the horse (above).

Tournament games were strictly managed by judges (left). A knight who had cheated or dishonoured another could be forced to sit out a melee and so lose.

Judges could stop a fight with the help of heralds or men-at-arms who would step in and force fighters apart.

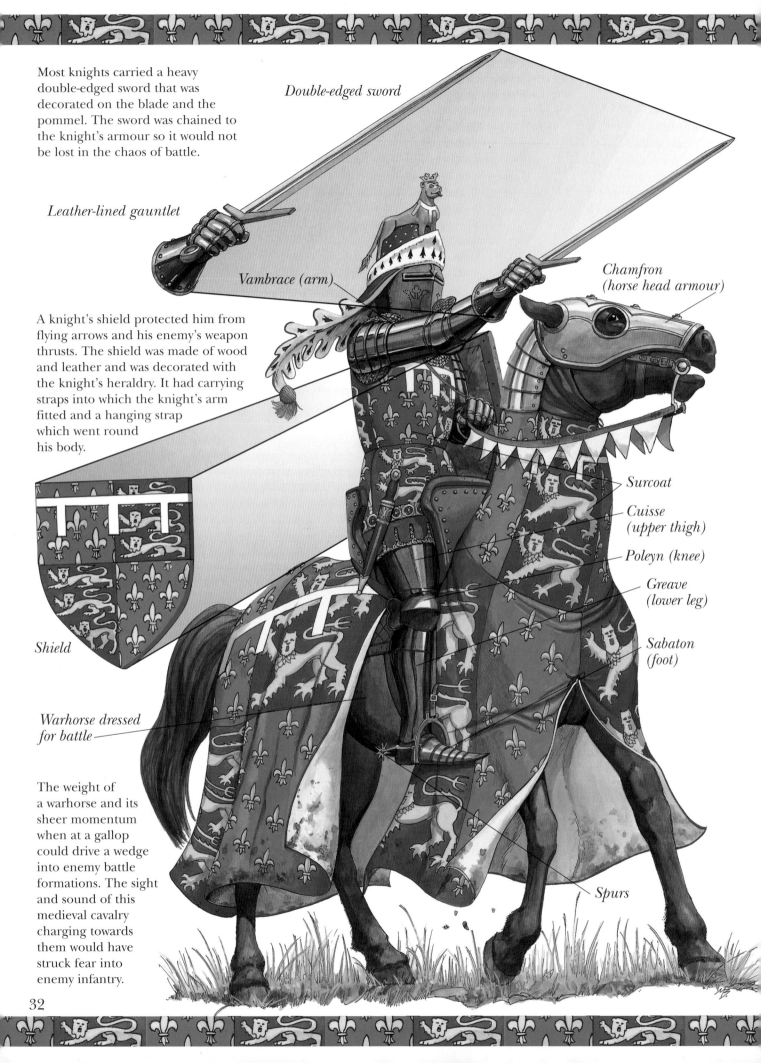

Most knights carried a heavy double-edged sword that was decorated on the blade and the pommel. The sword was chained to the knight's armour so it would not be lost in the chaos of battle.

Double-edged sword

Leather-lined gauntlet

Vambrace (arm)

Chamfron (horse head armour)

A knight's shield protected him from flying arrows and his enemy's weapon thrusts. The shield was made of wood and leather and was decorated with the knight's heraldry. It had carrying straps into which the knight's arm fitted and a hanging strap which went round his body.

Surcoat

Cuisse (upper thigh)

Poleyn (knee)

Greave (lower leg)

Sabaton (foot)

Shield

Warhorse dressed for battle

Spurs

The weight of a warhorse and its sheer momentum when at a gallop could drive a wedge into enemy battle formations. The sight and sound of this medieval cavalry charging towards them would have struck fear into enemy infantry.

Doublet
or aketon

Mail skirt attached

Plates of armour tied on

Helmet on last

It could take almost an hour to dress a knight in plate armour (above). Each separate piece had to be buckled and strapped, with hooks and latches, onto a cloth doublet, or aketon. The doublet had mail sewn onto the vulnerable areas of the body, such as around the groin and the armpits. The plates of armour were made to measure by the most skilful craftsmen. The helmet was the last piece of equipment to be put on.

READY FOR BATTLE

BETWEEN THE 11TH AND LATE 15TH CENTURIES armour changed enormously. Coats-of-mail used by the Normans around 1100 did not provide very good protection against a sharp sword point. The knights of the 13th century wore thickly-padded fabric over the top of the mail and extra solid-steel plates to protect legs, chest and arms. In the 1300s more plates were added to protect against different weapons. By the late 14th century knights were completely covered in this suit of plate armour that fitted together to protect the whole body. Helmets were designed to be smaller and lighter and shields also reduced in size. The best armour, made in Germany or Italy, was very expensive – a full set of armour and a warhorse cost the equivalent of a hundred years' wages for a common labourer!

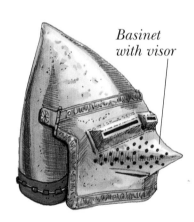

Basinet
with visor

This knight's helmet from the 14th century is called a basinet (above). It had a removeable visor that opened upwards. A wire-fixed, chain mail aventail, or neck guard, protected the wearer's neck. Narrow eye slits let the knight see and he was cooled by ventilation holes in the visor.

Fourteenth-century Italian knights (right) wore mail under their armour (a). The metal gloves, or gauntlets, were richly decorated (b), as were the buckles and hinges that held everything in place (c).

Italian knight c. 1385

UNDER ATTACK

Foot soldiers were easy targets for the well-trained archers on castle battlements

(a) (b) (c) (d)

CASTLES WERE ALMOST impossible to destroy until the invention of cannons in the 14th century. Until then, sieges were the preferred way to take control of enemy fortifications. A siege was a serious undertaking and could last for months, even years! If the defenders of the castle were persuaded to surrender with little resistance then this was not seen as shameful or dishonourable. In this event, the lives of the garrison and the castle inhabitants were spared. However, if the castle did not surrender, the outcome may have been a long and bloody battle. Often the castle occupants were starved into submission when the attackers cut off all supplies.

Archers used a variety of arrows to defeat the enemy. Bodkins (a) had fine, sharp points for piercing through the plate armour of knights. Broad-head arrows (b) were splayed and difficult to remove without worsening the injury – they were often used against horses. General purpose arrows (c) and (d) came in different weights and sizes.

In this scene, the attacking army has settled in for a long siege. They are also using siege towers, battering rams and trebuchet to break down the castle's defences (see page 36).

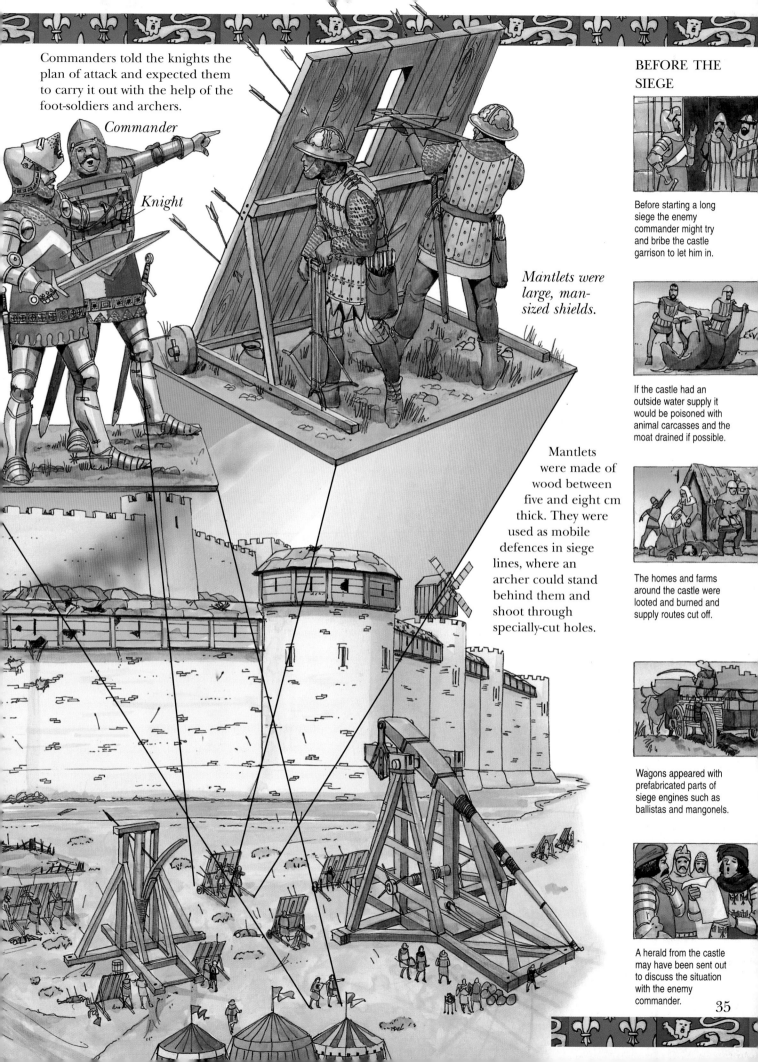

Commanders told the knights the plan of attack and expected them to carry it out with the help of the foot-soldiers and archers.

Commander

Knight

Mantlets were large, man-sized shields.

Mantlets were made of wood between five and eight cm thick. They were used as mobile defences in siege lines, where an archer could stand behind them and shoot through specially-cut holes.

BEFORE THE SIEGE

Before starting a long siege the enemy commander might try and bribe the castle garrison to let him in.

If the castle had an outside water supply it would be poisoned with animal carcasses and the moat drained if possible.

The homes and farms around the castle were looted and burned and supply routes cut off.

Wagons appeared with prefabricated parts of siege engines such as ballistas and mangonels.

A herald from the castle may have been sent out to discuss the situation with the enemy commander.

SIEGE WEAPONS

A N ATTACKING ARMY captured the surrounding land and cut off water and other supplies to a castle at the beginning of a siege. Then they pitched their tents and set up siege weapons. There were many methods of breaking down castle walls and many different weapons with which to do so. Artillery was used to hurl heavy stones at weak points in the castle defences. Fires lit against the walls heated and crumbled the mortar and stones making them weak. Tunnels were dug underneath walls too, in the hope that the tunnels would weaken the foundations and the castle walls would collapse.

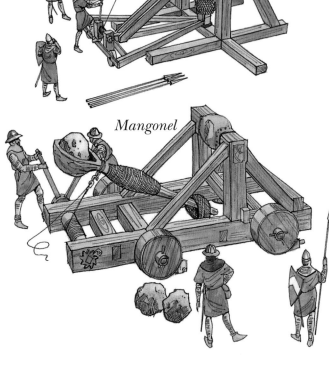

Ballista

Mangonel

Undermining of the castle may have been carried out during a long siege. After the moat was drained, tonnes of earth were moved and tunnels dug to get at the foundations of the castle walls. Once underneath, the attackers set light to the tunnel support timbers (below). When the supports and the tunnel collapsed, so did the wall above.

In hand-to-hand combat, one of the most effective weapons was a knight's sword. Castle staircases usually wound to the left. This allowed a defending soldier to thrust his right hand, holding his sword, forcing his enemy back down the stairs (left).

Undermining

The spring ballista (top) had a central lever which was drawn back almost to breaking point. When released, it shot a giant spear towards its target.

Mangonels (above) were first used by the ancient Romans and the design survived to the Middle Ages. Each mangonel had a huge wooden arm that was wound back under tension by a ratchet. When released, the rock in its cradle was hurled through the air.

Battering rams are among the oldest recorded siege weapons. They were made from a huge tree trunk with an iron tip. The men operating the weapon were sheltered from harm by a covering of hides. Teams of men repeatedly swung the battering rams to break the doors or walls of a castle.

Battering ram

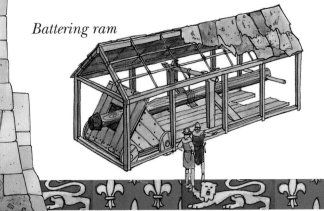

The trebuchet (right) was a fearsome weapon. Its throwing arm could send missiles flying over 200 m with incredible accuracy. The throwing arm was counter-balanced by a box full of rocks. Trebuchets were large machines and were either prefabricated or built on site by a specialist.

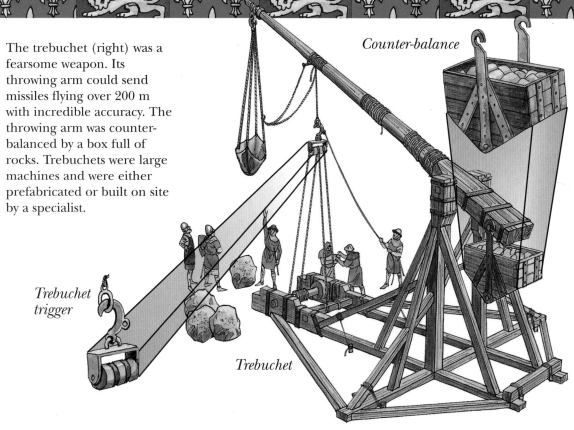

Counter-balance

Trebuchet trigger

Trebuchet

MISSILES

Missiles used by ballistas and trebuchets included the heads of local villagers or defenders. It was thought this would demoralise those inside the castle.

Dead and rotting animal carcasses were used to contaminate water and spread disease.

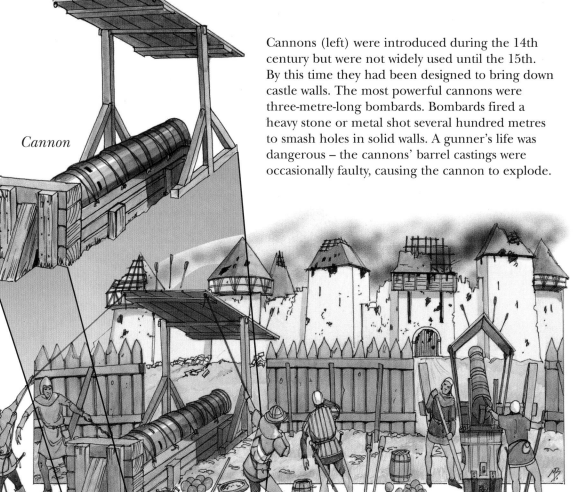

Cannon

Cannons (left) were introduced during the 14th century but were not widely used until the 15th. By this time they had been designed to bring down castle walls. The most powerful cannons were three-metre-long bombards. Bombards fired a heavy stone or metal shot several hundred metres to smash holes in solid walls. A gunner's life was dangerous – the cannons' barrel castings were occasionally faulty, causing the cannon to explode.

Ammunition for the largest trebuchets included rocks and stone balls, each weighing between 45 and 90kgs.

Fire pots smashed on impact and destroyed the dry wooden shingles (tiles) on the roofs of castle buildings (see page 38).

Siege tower

Preparing to
drop a fire pot

Castle defenders threw
fire pots – containers
filled with tar and oil
then set on fire – at the
attackers below. Fire
pots could also contain
boiling oil or water and
hot sand.

Women in the castle

Women may have acted
as nurses, helping the
chaplain and the
surgeon tend to the
dying and wounded.

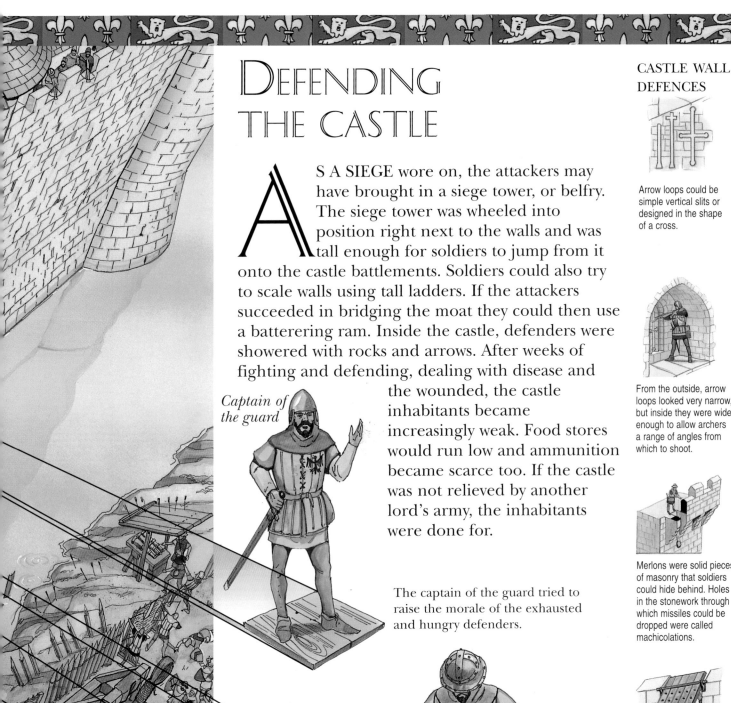

DEFENDING THE CASTLE

AS A SIEGE wore on, the attackers may have brought in a siege tower, or belfry. The siege tower was wheeled into position right next to the walls and was tall enough for soldiers to jump from it onto the castle battlements. Soldiers could also try to scale walls using tall ladders. If the attackers succeeded in bridging the moat they could then use a batterering ram. Inside the castle, defenders were showered with rocks and arrows. After weeks of fighting and defending, dealing with disease and the wounded, the castle inhabitants became increasingly weak. Food stores would run low and ammunition became scarce too. If the castle was not relieved by another lord's army, the inhabitants were done for.

Captain of the guard

The captain of the guard tried to raise the morale of the exhausted and hungry defenders.

Bowman

Bowmen sheltered behind battlements or arrow loops. Here they could take their time to shoot their crossbows accurately without exposing themselves to enemy fire.

The injured and wounded were laid on the floor (above) and tended by the castle surgeon. Wounds were cauterised with a red-hot iron. Cauterising burned off bad skin and stopped the bleeding.

Arrow loops could be simple vertical slits or designed in the shape of a cross.

From the outside, arrow loops looked very narrow, but inside they were wide enough to allow archers a range of angles from which to shoot.

Merlons were solid pieces of masonry that soldiers could hide behind. Holes in the stonework through which missiles could be dropped were called machicolations.

Wooden shutters were sometimes hung between merlons to provide extra protection to defending soldiers.

Brattices were wooden structures that overhung the walls. Soldiers used gaps in the brattice floor to rain missiles down on the enemy.

CASTLES AROUND THE WORLD

GREAT CASTLES have served as fortified homes and safe bases across the globe. From the graceful sloping roofs of a samurai castle to the massive red stone walls of a Mogul fortress, most castles reflect the architectural style and society of the period in which they were built. With the invention of the cannon in the 14th century, castles became of far less military importance – no castle could withstand a prolonged artillery bombardment from such weapons. Wars were increasingly fought by massed armies across whole countries, rather than between individual lords and barons. Society became more stable and trading generated wealth. Inherited titles, lands and fortunes were no longer the only source of riches and power.

Castrum was the Roman word for a fortified building and was the origin of the word 'castle'. The well-disciplined Roman army was able to build a wooden ditch and dike fort in just a few days when necessary. Some of these fortifications became permanent stone-built army bases.

Tower of London

Krak des Chevaliers (right), in Syria, is the most famous castle of the Crusades. It was occupied by the knights Hospitallers from 1109 until their surrender in 1271. Once the Saracens had captured the castle, they strengthened the outer wall.

Krak des Chevaliers

The White Tower (above) is the oldest part of the Tower of London. Its construction was started by the Normans in 1067.

The golden age of Japanese castle construction was between 1570 to 1690. Himeji Castle (left) was completed in 1609. This beautiful fortress was covered in intricately carved and painted wood.

Himeji Castle

Himeji was also known as White Egret Castle because its towers looked like birds in flight. A daimyo (warlord) built the castle on a grand scale to display his wealth and power.

The 13th-century castle of Chillon (right), in Switzerland, was built on an island in Lake Geneva that was the site of fortifications since ancient times. The castle's main purpose was to control shipping on the lake. Inside, the rooms were well furnished and the hall was brightly decorated with a fleur-de-lys design.

Chillon Castle

Fortress of Agra

The massive fortress of Agra (right), in India, has 2.5 km of surrounding walls that are over 21 m high. The Mogul conqueror Akbar (1542-1605) started the building and it was finished by his grandson. The fortress is three-sided and made of red sandstone.

Chateau Usse

Dornie Castle

Dornie Castle (above) stands isolated in the highlands of Scotland. It is a fine example of a fortified tower house, with water on all sides, making it easy to defend. It is linked to the mainland by a small bridge.

The Chateau Usse (above) is on the edge of the Forest of Chinon in the Loire Valley, France. Built on the foundations of another castle in 1485, the chateau is a good example of the Renaissance style and features luxurious interiors and fairy-tale turrets.

Neuschwanstein Castle

King Ludwig II of Bavaria built Neuschwanstein Castle (left) in Germany. It sits on top of a rocky outcrop high above the Lech Valley. This fairy-tale building was completed in 1886.

The British royal family still uses Windsor Castle (part of which is pictured below), England, as a family home. In 1992 a fire destroyed several of the rooms, including the chapel and banquet hall. These have been restored and are open to the public.

Windsor Castle

TIMESPAN

Some of the earliest known stone fortifications were at Mycenae in ancient Greece. They were destroyed in the fifth century BC and forgotten until they were discovered again in the 1800s. The fortifications were designed with a round tower surrounded by protective stone walls.

146 BC-AD 476 The Romans built many fortified towns and buildings all over their Empire, from Hadrian's Wall in Scotland to Amida in the Middle East. Most Roman forts were constructed to defend the Empire's frontiers. They differed slightly in shape and style, but their layout and buildings were of similar design.

AD 500-1000 The Byzantine Empire built many great fortifications, including the fourth-century Theodosian Wall and the palace at Constantinople (now known as Istanbul).

AD 774 The fortified stone palace of Isa Iba Musa in Ukheidur, near Baghdad in present-day Iraq, was far in advance of European wooden designs of the time.

AD 800 Feudalism began to form the structure of societies in western Europe.

AD 860s Viking slave merchants built well-defended round wooden forts to protect themselves against hostile locals.

AD 950 The earliest known French castle was built at Doue-La-Fontaine, Anjon.

1000 The great fortress at Telleborg in Denmark is believed to have been built for King Harald Bluetooth.

1066 William of Normandy invaded England and defeated King Harold. One of William's first acts was to erect a wooden castle at Hastings, which was later rebuilt in stone.

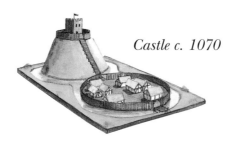
Castle c. 1070

1080s The first stone-built keeps were constructed. Around the 1100s these became the main strongholds of each castle.

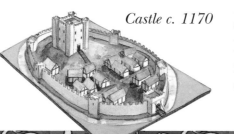
Castle c. 1170

1096 The Crusades start.

1140 The great tower at Hedingham Castle, in England, was finished. It is still standing today.

1150-1250s This was the main period of castle-building in England, France and Germany.

Captain of the guard

1198 Chateau Gaillard was built near Rouen, in France, overlooking the River Seine. It was built for King Richard I at great cost but features one of the best examples of corrugated curtain walls and had the first stone machicolations in Europe.

1205 Crusaders of the Order of Knights Hospitallers took over and rebuilt the castle of Krak des Chevaliers in Syria.

1266 King Edward I besieged Kenilworth Castle, in England. The castle did not succumb to the attack for a year due to its impressive defences. The castle's water defences made undermining impossible. The castle could only be bombarded by the longest-range weapons.

1271 Krak des Chevaliers falls to the Muslims.

1267-77 Caerphilly Castle in south Wales was built in a concentric design, with rings of stone walls inside each other. It was the largest castle in Wales.

c. 1280 Edward I built many huge castles in Wales to control the hostile Welsh. The castles were almost all concentric in design, including the castles at Beaumaris, Aberystwyth, Harlech and Rhuddlan.

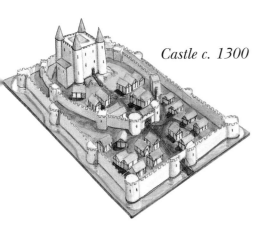

Castle c. 1300

c. 1320 Small cannons were first used in battle.

1337 The Hundred Years war began between France and England.

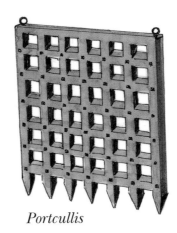

Portcullis

1345-51 An epidemic of the plague in Europe killed 25 million people.

c. 1350 The first castles to be built of brick were constructed in England and The Netherlands.

1400s Castle building declined in Europe.

1453 The Turks conquered the heavily fortified city of Constantinople (now Istanbul). Numerous guns were used to bombard the city walls from land and sea.

1475 The Spanish castle of Mazanareas El Real was built. It was an elaborately decorated castle – the towers were topped by stone cannon balls and fantastic machicolations. The machicolations were actually false and did not serve a military purpose.

c. 1530 Forts came to be used as gun platforms. King Henry VIII built Deal Castle in England for this purpose. It was designed with low, round walls. Many other fortifications had similar defences along the southern coast of England.

1570-1690 This period is now known as the golden age of samurai castle building in Japan. Matsumoto Castle (1596) had six levels in its keep.

1755 Stone forts in the shape of stars were built in Europe and America. They were built as gun platforms and, in this shape, fire from each gun could cover its neighbour. One of these forts, Fort Ticonderoga on the Canadian-American border was the source of an intense conflict between the British and the French before the American Revolution. The fort was also a strategic stronghold in the American Revolution itself.

c. 1800 The German fairy-tale castle of Neuschwanstein was built by King Ludwig of Bavaria.

Glossary

Aketon A padded garment worn underneath mail armour.

Armourer A metalworker who specialised in making armour and weapons.

Arrow loops Long narrow slits in a castle's walls from which arrows could be shot.

Artillery Military equipment such as guns, cannons and trebuchets.

Bailey The courtyard of a castle that included stables and other buildings.

Baron A medieval lord who oversaw large areas of land for the king.

Battering ram A large trunk of wood with a metal tip, used for knocking down castle gates.

Battlements Defensive stonework to protect soldiers on top of a castle's walls.

Bodkin An arrow head, usually triangular in shape for penetrating armour.

Bombardment A non-stop attack with cannons or catapults. A bombard was a heavy medieval cannon.

Borage A flowering plant whose leaves are sometimes used in salads or as seasoning.

Cauterise To burn the skin surrounding a wound in order to seal it.

Chivalry The knights' code of conduct.

Crossbow A very powerful bow that originated in the East. Early versions required soldiers to stretch them by hand in order to load them. In later models a mechanism was used to draw the bow and the arrows were called bolts or quarrels.

Crusades Wars during the 11th, 12th and 13th centuries between Christians and Muslims in the Holy Land.

Ewerer A servant whose duties included providing clean cloths for the meal tables.

Falconer A servant in charge of training birds of prey for hunting.

Feudal system The organisation of society in medieval times.

Fleur-de-Lys A heraldic symbol of a lily with three distinct petals.

Garrison A group of soldiers who guarded a castle.

Heraldry The system of symbols and colours on shields and flags identifying noble families.

Jester A man who kept the castle household entertained by telling jokes and making faces.

Machicolations Stone constructions overhanging the castle walls from which objects could be dropped.

Manor The manor house or castle of a lord and the lands attached to it.

Men-at-arms Fully-armed guards who would step in to control tournament fighters with their staffs when necessary.

Middle Ages Another term for medieval times, the period between about AD 1000 and 1450.

Moat A deep water-filled ditch around a castle that was an important defence against enemies.

Plate armour Armour made up of body-hugging sheets of metal. It was also known as white armour.

Pommel The raised part at the front of a saddle.

Prefabricated To make something in sections so it can be easily transported to and assembled on a site.

Quintain An apparatus for training to joust with a lance.

Samurai The Japanese fighting class equivalent to the European knights of the Middle Ages.

Slander Any false or insulting thing spoken about another person.

Spur A spiky attachment fitted to the heel of a horseback rider, used to make the horse speed up.

Tallow A waxy material made from animal bones and sheep fat.

Trencher A large slice of stale bread used as a plate in the Middle Ages. Later, the word was used to mean a plate made from metal or wood.

Vestments Ceremonial garments worn by a chaplain during religious services.

INDEX Page numbers in bold refer to illustrations

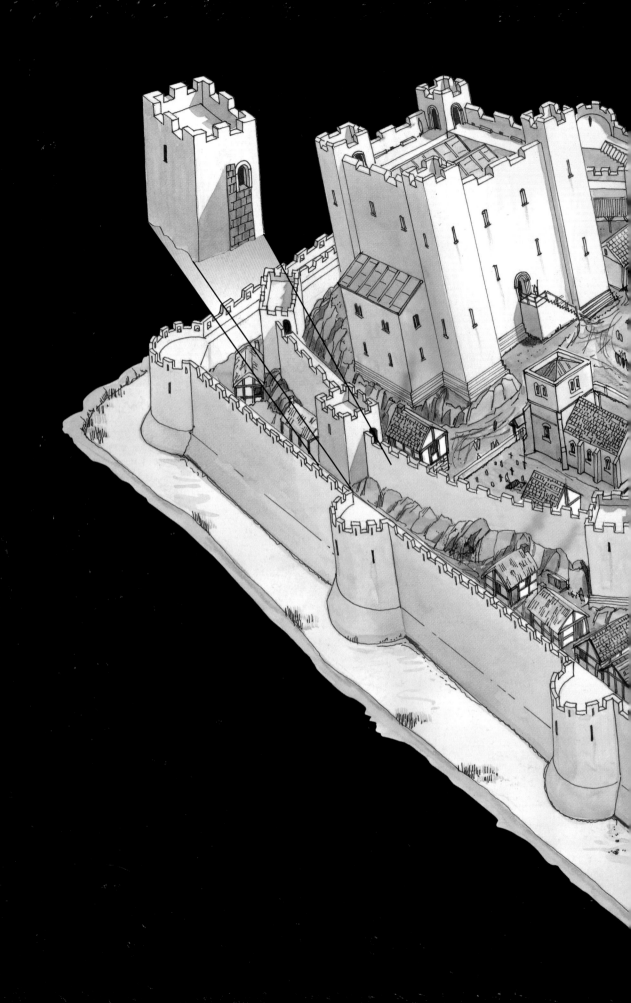